pull-aparts

pull. eat. repeat.

HANDY TOOLS

Cut clumps of dough with **kitchen shears** or a **sharp knife**.

Flatten dough with a **rolling pin** or your **hands**.

Use a **pizza cutter** to slice flattened dough easily.

Wrap **thread** or plain **dental floss** around a dough log and pull slowly to slice nice even rounds.

Printed in the United States of America
by G&R Publishing Co.

Distributed By:

507 Industrial Street
Waverly, IA 50677

ISBN-13: 978-1-56383-538-4
Item #7124

PULL. EAT. REPEAT.

Whether stacked, stuffed, layered, or sliced, these pull-apart breads are a fun way to serve and eat appetizers, meals, or desserts. Just pull off a piece, devour, and grab another! Here are some tips to make preparation fast and easy.

1 Thaw frozen dough in a greased pan in the refrigerator for 4 to 8 hours or overnight for no-fuss assembly later. If cutting is required, handle the dough when it's still cold; if you're flattening the dough, set it out at room temperature for 30 minutes first so it will stretch more easily. If dough springs back during rolling, simply let it rest a few more minutes.

2 To prevent dough from sticking, lightly coat your work surface with flour.

3 To let bread rise, leave the oven off and place a pan of hot water on the lower rack; set the pan of bread on the top rack. Cover with sprayed waxed paper and drape a lightweight towel over the top to capture the moist heat. *(Be sure to uncover before baking.)*

4 If bread is browning too quickly as it bakes, cover loosely with foil *(like a tent)* or shield just the edges, which tend to brown first.

5 Be sure to use the type of yeast called for in recipes and mix as directed because active dry and instant/quick-rise yeasts are incorporated differently.

4

STUFFED PIZZA BITES

¼ C. pizza sauce, plus more for dipping

1¼ C. shredded mozzarella cheese

1 (13.8 oz.) tube refrigerated "classic" pizza dough

½ C. chopped pepperoni

Other diced toppings as desired *(such as bell peppers)*

2 T. butter, melted

1 tsp. garlic powder

1 tsp. Italian seasoning

3 T. grated Parmesan cheese

TO BEGIN, preheat the oven to 400°. Grease a 9" pie plate with cooking spray.

In a small bowl, mix ¼ cup pizza sauce and mozzarella cheese. Unroll the dough and press it into an 8 x 12" rectangle. Slice dough into 24 (2") squares. Divide the cheese mixture evenly among the squares. Add the pepperoni and other toppings, if you'd like. Gather the sides of each square together and pinch the dough to enclose fillings and form a ball. Place them seam side down in the prepared pie plate.

In a small bowl, mix melted butter, garlic powder, and Italian seasoning; brush over the dough. Sprinkle evenly with Parmesan cheese. Bake 20 to 25 minutes or until golden brown and baked through.

SERVE PROMPTLY with extra pizza sauce.

Pull-Aparts

5

CARAMEL SKILLET
S'mores

1 (11 oz.) tube refrigerated French bread dough

3 T. sugar

½ C. graham cracker crumbs

½ C. butter, divided

1½ C. mini marshmallows

1 (8 oz.) pkg. mini Rolos candies

¼ C. chopped pecans

TO BEGIN, preheat the oven to 350°. Slice the loaf of dough into 10 rounds. Cut each round into four equal pieces. In a large zippered plastic bag, mix the sugar and cracker crumbs; set aside.

Place a 10" oven-proof skillet over low heat and melt 5 tablespoons butter; swirl the skillet to coat the bottom of pan. Remove from heat and set aside.

Melt the remaining 3 tablespoons butter in the microwave. Working with a few dough pieces at a time, dip them in melted butter and then coat in the set-aside crumb mixture. Arrange all coated pieces in the buttered skillet. Top with marshmallows and candies, pressing them gently into the dough. Sprinkle with pecans. Bake about 25 minutes or until bread is done. Cool slightly before serving.

TRY mini Reese's Peanut Butter Cups in place of Rolos and chopped peanuts in place of pecans for a perfectly nutty s'more.

Pull-Aparts

6

7

Piña Colada Ring

½ C. butter

¼ C. milk

1 tsp. coconut flavoring

1¾ C. sugar

2 (16.3 oz.) tubes refrigerated "grands" flaky biscuits *(8 ct. each)*

1 (20 oz.) can crushed pineapple, drained *(reserve juice for glaze)*

Coconut Glaze *(recipe follows)*

¼ C. chopped dried pineapple

Sweetened flaked coconut

Maraschino cherries

8

TO BEGIN, preheat the oven to 350°. Grease a 10" Bundt pan with cooking spray and set aside.

In a small saucepan over medium-low heat, combine the butter and milk; heat and stir until butter melts and mixture is smooth. Remove from heat; stir in coconut flavoring and set aside. Pour sugar into a bowl.

Cut each biscuit into four equal pieces. Dip each piece into the butter mixture and then roll in sugar. Arrange 21 of the coated biscuit pieces evenly in the prepared pan and top with half the crushed pineapple. Make another layer of 21 coated biscuits and the rest of the pineapple. Arrange remaining 22 biscuits over the top. Set the pan on a rimmed baking sheet and bake 40 to 45 minutes or until deep golden brown and baked through. Tent bread with foil toward the end of baking time to prevent overbrowning.

Cool for 10 minutes before inverting onto a serving plate. Drizzle Coconut Glaze over warm bread and top with dried pineapple, some coconut, and a few cherries.

COCONUT GLAZE
Whisk together a generous 1 C. powdered sugar, 2½ T. reserved pineapple juice, and ½ tsp. coconut flavoring until smooth.

REUBEN PULLS

8 oz. corned beef or pastrami, thinly sliced

8 oz. baby Swiss cheese, thinly sliced

1 round loaf sourdough bread, unsliced

½ C. Thousand Island dressing, plus more for serving

1 (8 oz.) can sauerkraut, drained & warmed

Caraway seed, optional

TO BEGIN, preheat the oven to 375°. Cut beef and cheese into bite-size pieces and set aside.

Cut the bread into 1" slices in one direction without cutting through the bottom crust. Spread dressing on both sides of each slice. Cut the bread in the opposite direction in 1" slices, again without cutting through the bottom crust. Set the loaf on a large piece of foil and spread more dressing between the new cuts.

Stuff beef and cheese into all the cuts, pressing some down into the loaf and arranging some toward the top so it's fully loaded. Wrap the loaf in foil and set it on a cookie sheet. Bake 15 minutes or until hot and melty. Open foil to uncover the bread; bake 5 to 7 minutes longer. Top with some sauerkraut and sprinkle with caraway seed, if you'd like.

SERVE WARM with Thousand Island dressing and more sauerkraut.

TRY rye or marble bread, or stuff this loaf with other favorite meats and cheeses.

11

12

MEAT-LOVERS'
Breakfast Bake

10 bacon strips, chopped

1 lb. breakfast sausage

2 (16 oz.) tubes refrigerated "grands" buttermilk biscuits *(8 ct. each)*

3 T. butter

1 to 2 tsp. minced garlic

2 C. shredded Mexican 4-cheese blend, or more to taste

TO BEGIN, preheat the oven to 375°. Generously grease a 12" oven-safe skillet with cooking spray and set aside.

In another skillet over medium heat, partially cook the bacon; add the sausage and cook until crumbly. Drain meat on paper towels and discard the grease.

Cut each biscuit into four equal pieces. Flatten the pieces and put a spoonful of meat mixture in the center of each one. Pinch the edges together to seal filling inside and shape each one into a ball. Arrange them seam side down in the prepared skillet with edges touching *(they'll be cozy).*

Melt butter in the microwave and stir in the garlic. Brush the butter mixture over the dough. Sprinkle cheese on top. Bake about 30 minutes or until edges are golden brown and cheese is melted. Serve promptly.

Pull-Aparts

13

MAPLE CARAMEL
Bubble Bread

½ C. raisins

2 T. flour

½ C. finely chopped pecans

¼ C. sugar

1 tsp. cinnamon

2 T. beaten egg or egg substitute

¼ C. butter, softened, divided

¼ C. pure maple syrup

1 T. light corn syrup

¼ C. brown sugar

1 (1 lb.) loaf frozen white bread dough, thawed

Maple Icing *(recipe follows)*

TO BEGIN, lightly grease an 8 x 8" baking pan with cooking spray and line with buttered parchment paper. Soak raisins in hot water until plump, 5 to 10 minutes; drain well.

For the filling, stir together flour, pecans, sugar, cinnamon, egg, and 3 tablespoons butter; set aside.

In a small saucepan over medium heat, combine the maple syrup, corn syrup, brown sugar, and remaining 1 tablespoon butter. Bring to a boil; stir, reduce heat, and simmer for 3 minutes. Remove from heat and cool slightly; pour into prepared pan and set aside.

On a lightly floured surface, roll dough into an 8 x 14" rectangle. Spread set-aside filling over dough and sprinkle with plumped raisins. Starting at one long edge, roll dough

DIRECTIONS CONTINUED ·······························>

Pull-Aparts

14

into a log; pinch to seal. Cut log crosswise into 2" pieces and then cut pieces in half. Fit the pieces into prepared pan randomly. Cover with sprayed waxed paper and let rise in a warm place about 1 hour.

Preheat the oven to 350°. Bake 45 to 50 minutes or until center is done. Cool for 10 minutes before removing from pan. Drizzle with Maple Icing.

MAPLE ICING Whisk

together 2 T. melted butter, 1 C. powdered sugar, ½ tsp. maple flavoring, and just enough milk to make a smooth icing.

16

PB Muffins

2½ C. bread flour, divided*

¼ C. sugar

2¼ tsp. instant quick-rise yeast *(not active dry)*

⅓ C. milk

⅓ C. plus 1 T. creamy peanut butter, divided

¼ C. warm water *(120°)*

2 eggs

1 tsp. vanilla

½ tsp. salt

3 T. butter

¼ C. brown sugar

Peanut Butter Frosting *(recipe follows)*

Coarsely crushed honey-roasted peanuts

* You may also use all-purpose flour.

TO BEGIN, grease 12 standard muffin cups and set aside. In a large mixing bowl, mix 1 cup flour, sugar, and yeast. Beat in milk, ⅓ cup peanut butter, and warm water on medium speed until well blended. Beat in the eggs one at a time. Stir in vanilla, salt, and 1¼ cups additional flour. Knead with an electric mixer and dough hook *(or by hand)* for 8 to 10 minutes, adding the last ¼ cup flour gradually until dough is soft and only slightly sticky. On a floured board, shape dough into a ball; place in a greased bowl, cover with sprayed waxed paper, and let rise in a warm place 1 hour or until doubled in size.

Punch dough down and knead twice. On a lightly floured surface, roll dough into a 15 x 20" rectangle.

For filling, warm the butter and remaining 1 tablespoon peanut butter in the microwave; stir until smooth. Brush over dough and sprinkle with brown sugar. Slice dough lengthwise to make 10 (1½ x 20") strips. Cut dough in half crosswise for 20 total strips. Stack strips together in groups of five and cut each stack into three equal bundles (3½" to 4" long). On each bundle, flip the top piece over, filling side down. Set one bundle into each prepared muffin cup, long edges up. Cover with sprayed waxed paper and let rise in a warm place about 30 minutes.

Preheat the oven to 350°. Bake about 15 minutes or until golden brown. Cool slightly; frost and top with peanuts.

PEANUT BUTTER FROSTING Microwave

2½ T. cream cheese and 1½ T. creamy peanut butter until softened. Stir in 6 T. powdered sugar and 3½ T. half & half until creamy.

17

BBQ CHICKEN
Ranch Ring

2 (11 oz.) tubes refrigerated "original" breadstick dough *(12 ct. each)*

3 T. butter, melted

Dried dill weed

1¼ C. shredded cooked chicken

⅓ C. barbecue sauce

¼ C. ranch dressing, plus more for dipping

½ C. cooked crumbled bacon

1½ C. shredded smoked cheddar cheese

TO BEGIN, preheat the oven to 375°. Grease a 12" pizza pan and the outside of a 4" oven-safe bowl with cooking spray. Set the bowl upside down in the center of prepared pan and set aside.

Unroll dough and separate all the breadsticks. Flatten each one until about 1½" wide; brush with melted butter and sprinkle with dill weed. Cut the breadsticks in half crosswise and roll each piece into a loose coil. Set the coils upright on the prepared pan *(around the bowl)*. Flatten the coils with the bottom of a greased drinking glass until they fill the pan and create a "crust" *(don't worry if there are a few openings between coils)*. Bake the crust about 18 minutes, until light golden brown and firm to the touch.

DIRECTIONS CONTINUED ·····························>

Pull-Aparts

18

While the crust bakes, combine the chicken and barbecue sauce in a small saucepan over low heat, stirring several times; keep warm. Remove crust from oven and reduce oven temperature to 350°. Brush ¼ cup ranch dressing over the warm crust and sprinkle evenly with bacon. Spread the chicken mixture on top and sprinkle with cheese. Return pan to oven to bake 7 to 10 minutes more, until cheese melts and crust is done. Carefully remove the hot bowl.

SERVE WITH ranch dressing.

19

LEMONY LAYERS

7 T. sugar

1 tsp. poppy seed

Zest from 1 lemon
(use juice for glaze)

1 (8 oz.) tube refrigerated "grands" flaky biscuits *(8 ct.)*

3 T. butter, melted

Creamy Lemon Glaze *(recipe follows)*

TO BEGIN, preheat the oven to 350°. Grease a 3½ x 7" loaf pan with cooking spray and line with parchment paper, allowing an overhang on long sides.

In a small bowl, mix the sugar, poppy seed, and lemon zest *(about 2 teaspoons)*. Split each biscuit into two round layers. Brush both sides of each layer with melted butter and coat well in sugar mixture. Set biscuit layers on edge in pan until filled *(they'll fit snugly)*. Sprinkle any remaining sugar mixture between the biscuits and over the top.

Bake 30 to 40 minutes or until golden brown and done in the center. Tent with foil partway through baking time to prevent overbrowning. Cool 10 minutes before lifting bread from pan. Drizzle with Creamy Lemon Glaze.

CREAMY LEMON GLAZE
Juice the zested lemon. Beat together 1 T. softened cream cheese, 1½ T. melted butter, ½ C. powdered sugar, and 1 to 2 T. lemon juice until smooth.

Pull-Aparts

Cheesy Mushroom Pulls

2 T. plus ½ C. butter, divided

12 oz. fresh mushrooms, sliced

1 T. chopped fresh thyme

1 round loaf 7-grain bread, unsliced

8 oz. provolone cheese, thinly sliced

4 oz. American cheese, thinly sliced

½ C. diced green onions

1½ tsp. poppy seed

22

TO BEGIN, preheat the oven to 350°.

Melt 2 tablespoons butter in a medium skillet over medium heat. Add the mushrooms and cook 4 to 5 minutes, stirring often *(mushrooms will give off moisture)*. Stir in the thyme and cook 2 to 3 minutes more. Set aside to cool.

Cut the bread into ¾" slices in one direction without cutting through the bottom crust. Then cut the bread in the opposite direction using the same method to make cube-shaped pieces. Set the loaf on a large piece of foil. Insert pieces of provolone cheese between the cuts and then add the mushrooms and any juices, pressing some down into the loaf. Fill in the spaces with pieces of American cheese.

Melt the remaining ½ cup butter in the microwave. Stir in the green onions and poppy seed. Drizzle the mixture evenly over bread and between cuts. Wrap the loaf in foil and set it on a cookie sheet. Bake for 15 minutes. Open foil to uncover the bread and bake about 12 minutes longer or until cheese is melted.

SERVE WARM.

STRAWBERRY
Cheesecake Ring

¾ C. graham cracker crumbs

¾ C. sugar

½ C. plus 2 T. butter, divided

2 (16.3 oz.) tubes refrigerated "grands" flaky biscuits *(8 ct. each)*

1 (21 oz.) can strawberry pie filling

1 C. white chocolate chips

Cream Cheese Icing *(recipe follows)*

TO BEGIN, preheat the oven to 350°. Generously grease a 10" Bundt pan with cooking spray. In a large zippered plastic bag, mix cracker crumbs and sugar; melt ½ cup butter in a bowl and set all aside.

Cut each biscuit into six equal pieces. Dip the pieces in melted butter, a few at a time, and drop into the crumbs; seal the bag and shake to coat. Set pieces aside. In a medium saucepan over medium-low heat, mix pie filling and remaining 2 tablespoons butter. Bring to a low boil and stir for 1 to 2 minutes; remove from heat.

To assemble, arrange 32 coated biscuit pieces in the bottom of prepared pan. Spoon half the strawberry filling over the dough and sprinkle with half the white chocolate chips. Layer with 32 more pieces of

DIRECTIONS CONTINUED ·······························>

Pull-Aparts

24

dough, remaining filling, and remaining chips. Top with remaining biscuit pieces.

Bake about 50 minutes or until golden brown and done in the center. Cool 10 to 15 minutes before inverting onto a serving plate. Spread Cream Cheese Icing on top and serve warm.

CREAM CHEESE ICING

With an electric mixer, beat together ¾ C. powdered sugar, 3 oz. softened cream cheese, 1½ T. milk, and ½ tsp. lemon juice until smooth.

MONTE CRISTO

1 (1 lb.) loaf frozen white bread dough, thawed

2 T. butter, melted

12 Swiss cheese slices, halved

12 thin ham slices *(about 8 oz.)*

12 thin turkey slices *(about 8 oz.)*

TO BEGIN, generously grease a 5 x 9" loaf pan with cooking spray and line with parchment paper, allowing an overhang on long sides; set aside.

On a lightly floured surface, roll dough into a 12 x 20" rectangle. Slice the dough lengthwise into 3 (4") strips. Brush dough with melted butter. Cut dough crosswise into 8 (2") strips to make 24 (2 x 4") rectangles.

To assemble, set the prepared pan up on one short side. Layer one piece each of dough, cheese, and ham, followed by one piece each of dough, cheese, and turkey. Repeat the layers until pan is filled, ending with a piece of dough. Turn the pan upright and cover with sprayed waxed paper; let rise in a warm place about 1 hour.

Preheat the oven to 350°. Bake about 35 minutes, covering loosely with foil partway through baking time to prevent overbrowning. Let cool 15 minutes and then remove from pan.

SERVE WARM with a dusting of powdered sugar and a side of raspberry jam.

Pull-Aparts

BUFFALO CHICKEN
Pockets

6 T. butter, melted

¼ C. buffalo wing sauce

¼ tsp. garlic powder

⅛ tsp. salt

1½ C. shredded cooked chicken

¼ C. chopped green onions

2 (8 oz.) tubes seamless crescent dough sheet

½ C. crumbled blue cheese, divided

½ C. shredded cheddar cheese, divided

TO BEGIN, preheat the oven to 350°. Grease an 8 x 8" baking dish with cooking spray and line with parchment paper. In one bowl, mix butter, sauce, garlic powder, and salt. In another bowl, combine chicken, green onions, and 3 tablespoons of the butter mixture; set everything aside.

On a floured board, unroll and flatten each sheet of dough. Slice each one in half lengthwise and into four even crosswise strips to get eight pieces per sheet. Place some chicken mixture in the center of each piece. Sprinkle half each of the blue cheese and cheddar cheese over chicken and press down lightly. Fold each piece in half to enclose filling; seal cut edges together with a fork.

Set "pockets" in rows in prepared pan, sealed edges up. Drizzle with remaining butter mixture and sprinkle with remaining cheeses. Bake 30 to 35 minutes or until golden brown. Let cool 10 minutes before removing from pan.

SERVE WITH blue cheese or ranch dressing.

Pull-Aparts

28

SWEET APPLE BITES

1 (16.3 oz.) tube refrigerated "grands" homestyle buttermilk biscuits *(8 ct.)*

¼ C. butter

¼ C. brown sugar, divided

1½ tsp. cinnamon, divided

2 apples, cored & diced

½ C. half & half

1 egg yolk

½ C. caramel topping

½ tsp. coarse salt, optional

Vanilla Icing *(recipe follows)*

TO BEGIN, preheat the oven to 350°. Cut each biscuit into eight equal pieces and set aside.

In a 12" oven-proof skillet over medium heat, melt the butter. Add 2 tablespoons brown sugar, 1 teaspoon cinnamon, and apples; stir and cook for 5 minutes. Add biscuit pieces to skillet and stir gently into apple mixture. Remove from heat.

In a large spouted measuring cup, combine half & half, egg yolk, remaining 2 tablespoons brown sugar, and remaining ½ teaspoon cinnamon; whisk well. Drizzle over biscuit mixture in skillet and press down lightly.

Bake 25 to 30 minutes or until biscuits are golden brown and apples are tender. Remove from oven; drizzle with caramel and sprinkle with coarse salt, if you'd like. Drizzle Vanilla Icing over everything. Serve warm.

VANILLA ICING Whisk together 1 C. powdered sugar, 1 tsp. vanilla, and 3 to 4 T. heavy cream until smooth.

Pull-Aparts

31

Lemon Blueberry Stack

1 (1 lb.) loaf frozen sweet dough, thawed*

½ C. sugar

2 T. lemon zest

1 T. orange zest

¼ C. butter, melted

1 C. fresh blueberries

Cream Cheese Icing *(recipe follows)*

* Let thawed dough rest at room temperature for 30 minutes before rolling out.

32

TO BEGIN, grease a 5 x 9" loaf pan with cooking spray and set aside.

On a lightly floured surface, roll dough into a 12 x 20" rectangle. In a small bowl, stir together the sugar, lemon zest, and orange zest; set aside.

Brush melted butter over dough and sprinkle with sugar mixture. Cut dough crosswise into 5 (4 x 12") strips. Then slice the dough lengthwise into 6 (2") strips to make 30 (2 x 4") pieces. Stack pieces together in groups of five to get six bundles. Set the prepared pan up on one short side and stack the bundles in pan with the filling side up *(there will be extra space)*. Flip the last piece over, filling side down. Turn the pan upright and arrange dough pieces more evenly. Press a few blueberries between each layer. Cover with sprayed waxed paper and let rise in a warm place 40 to 50 minutes or until doubled in size.

Preheat the oven to 350°. Bake 30 to 40 minutes or until golden brown and done in the center. Tent with foil as needed to prevent overbrowning. Let cool for 10 minutes before removing from pan. Frost with Cream Cheese Icing.

CREAM CHEESE ICING Beat together 3 oz. softened cream cheese, ⅓ C. powdered sugar, and 1 to 2 T. lemon juice until smooth and spreadable.

33

SAUSAGE-STUFFED
Cinnamon Rolls

2 (12.4 oz.) tube refrigerated cinnamon rolls with frosting *(8 ct. each)*

½ C. sugar

½ tsp. cinnamon

32 cocktail sausages *(like Lil' Smokies)*

16 (¼"-thick) slices smoked Swiss & cheddar cheese, halved

TO BEGIN, preheat the oven to 350°. Generously grease a 10" Bundt pan with cooking spray.

Separate the rolls and set frosting containers out. In a small bowl, mix the sugar and cinnamon; set aside.

Carefully slice each roll in half horizontally to make two round disks. Use a rolling pin to flatten each disk into a 4" circle. Place one sausage and one piece of cheese in the center of each dough circle. Wrap dough around filling to make a bundle, pinching well to seal. Roll the bundles in the set-aside sugar mixture and arrange evenly in prepared pan, seam side down.

Bake about 30 minutes or until golden brown and cooked through. Let cool 5 minutes before inverting onto a serving plate. Drizzle with the set-aside frosting.

SERVE WITH maple syrup, if you'd like.

CAPRESE BREAD

15 to 18 frozen white dinner rolls, thawed but still cold

3 T. olive oil

¼ C. finely chopped fresh basil, plus more for sprinkling

1½ tsp. minced garlic

½ tsp. garlic salt

Black pepper to taste

4 oz. mozzarella cheese, cubed, divided

2 Roma tomatoes, chopped & seeded, divided

Coarse salt

TO BEGIN, generously grease a 5 x 9" loaf pan with cooking spray. Cut each roll into four even pieces and set aside.

In a small bowl, stir together the oil, ¼ cup basil, garlic, garlic salt, and pepper. Dip dough pieces into oil mixture to coat and layer half the pieces in prepared pan. Arrange about ⅓ each of the cheese cubes and tomatoes between the dough pieces; top with the remaining dough. Cover pan with sprayed waxed paper and let rise in a warm place until doubled in size, about 1 hour.

Preheat the oven to 350°. Press the remaining cheese cubes and tomatoes into the crevices between dough pieces. Set the pan on a cookie sheet and bake 25 to 35 minutes or until golden brown and done in the center. Sprinkle with coarse salt and additional basil.

SERVE WARM.

38

Skillet Rolls & Dip

Vegetable oil

12 to 14 frozen white dinner rolls, thawed but still cold

4 C. loosely packed fresh baby spinach, chopped

1 (6.5 oz.) jar marinated artichoke hearts, drained & chopped

4 oz. cream cheese, softened

½ C. sour cream

¼ C. mayonnaise

½ tsp. minced garlic

½ tsp. Sriracha or hot sauce

¼ C. grated Parmesan cheese

½ C. shredded mozzarella cheese, divided

Salt and black pepper

2 T. butter, melted

Coarse salt

TO BEGIN, generously oil a 10" oven-safe skillet and the outside of a 4½" oven-safe bowl. Set the bowl upside down in the center of skillet and arrange the rolls snugly around the edge. With kitchen shears, snip an "X" in the top of each roll. Cover with sprayed waxed paper and let rolls rise in a warm place for 1 hour or until doubled in size.

Meanwhile, make the dip. Combine spinach and 1 tablespoon water in a medium microwave-safe bowl; cover and microwave on high for 1 minute. Let stand 15 minutes. Drain spinach; add the artichokes, cream cheese, sour cream, mayonnaise, garlic, Sriracha sauce, Parmesan cheese, and ¼ cup mozzarella cheese. Season with salt and pepper; mix well. Cover and refrigerate until needed.

When rolls have risen, preheat the oven to 375°. Brush tops with melted butter and sprinkle with coarse salt. Remove bowl from skillet and spoon prepared dip into the center space, pushing it against the dough. Sprinkle remaining ¼ cup mozzarella cheese over the dip. Bake 25 to 30 minutes, until rolls are golden brown and sound hollow when tapped and dip is bubbly. Let cool 5 to 10 minutes before serving.

PEACHY CINNAMON
Mini Loaves

½ C. chopped peaches *(we used canned)*

1 tsp. vanilla

1½ T. butter, softened

2 T. sugar

¼ C. brown sugar

¾ tsp. cinnamon, divided

Dash of ground nutmeg

1 (8 oz.) tube seamless crescent dough sheet

¼ C. chopped pecans

Glaze *(recipe below)*

TO BEGIN, preheat the oven to 350°. Generously grease four mini loaf pans with cooking spray. *(Ours were 2¼ x 4" but you can also use one standard loaf pan.)* Toss the peaches with vanilla and set aside.

To make the filling, mix butter, sugar, brown sugar, ½ teaspoon cinnamon, and nutmeg. Unroll dough on a lightly floured surface and flatten to make a 10 x 13" rectangle. Spread filling evenly over dough. Thoroughly drain the peaches and scatter them over the filling. Sprinkle with pecans.

Slice dough into small rectangles that will fit your pan when stacked. *(We cut five lengthwise rows and nine crosswise rows to make pieces about 1½ x 2".)* Set a loaf pan up on one short side and stack 11 or 12 pieces in the pan with the filling side up; flip the last piece over, filling side down. Turn the pan upright. Fill remaining pans the same way.

DIRECTIONS CONTINUED ·······························>

Pull-Aparts

40

Set pans on a cookie sheet and bake 25 to 30 minutes or until golden brown and done in the center. Cool slightly and remove from pans. Drizzle with Glaze and serve warm.

GLAZE Whisk together 1 C. powdered sugar, a splash of vanilla, and 2 to 3 tsp. milk until smooth.

TRY diced apples in place of the peaches and walnuts in place of pecans for autumn deliciousness.

41

HONEY-ORANGE
Pulls

½ C. butter, softened

¼ C. powdered sugar

¼ C. honey

1 tsp. vanilla

Zest from 1 orange
(use juice for glaze)

1 round loaf ciabatta
bread, unsliced

3 T. sugar

½ C. finely chopped
macadamia nuts

Orange Glaze
(recipe follows)

TO BEGIN, preheat the oven to 350°. In a small mixing bowl, beat together the butter and powdered sugar until smooth. Stir in the honey, vanilla, and orange zest; set aside.

Cut bread into ¾" slices in one direction without cutting through the bottom crust. Then slice the loaf diagonally using the same method to make diamond-shaped pieces. Set the loaf on a large piece of foil. Spread set-aside butter mixture on all cut sides. In a small bowl, mix the sugar and nuts; sprinkle generously between all cuts.

Wrap the loaf in foil and set it on a cookie sheet. Bake 25 to 30 minutes or until bread is warm. Open foil to uncover the bread; bake 5 to 8 minutes more, until lightly browned. Drizzle with Orange Glaze and serve promptly.

ORANGE GLAZE Juice the zested orange. Whisk
together 1 C. powdered sugar, 2 T. orange juice, ¼ tsp. orange flavoring, 1 T. honey, and a pinch of salt until smooth.

STEAK FAJITA BAKE

1 (12 oz.) tube refrigerated Texas-style biscuits *(10 ct.)*

1 (1.12 oz.) pkg. fajita seasoning mix, divided

1 C. diced bell peppers *(red, green, or both)*

½ C. diced onion

1 T. vegetable oil

1 lb. beef sirloin steak, thinly sliced

½ C. water

2 C. shredded Colby-Jack cheese

TO BEGIN, preheat the oven to 375°. Grease a 9 x 13" baking dish with cooking spray and set aside.

Cut each biscuit into four even pieces. Place all pieces in a medium bowl and sprinkle with 1 tablespoon seasoning mix; toss to coat well and set aside.

In a large skillet over medium-high heat, cook peppers and onion for 3 to 5 minutes, stirring occasionally; transfer to a plate to keep warm. Add oil to the skillet and cook steak strips until browned. Sprinkle remaining seasoning mix over meat and add the water; cook and stir until sauce is thickened. Return vegetables to skillet and stir well. Spread steak mixture in prepared baking dish and arrange biscuit pieces on top.

Bake for 20 minutes or until biscuits are light golden brown. Sprinkle with cheese and bake 5 minutes more, until cheese is melted.

SERVE WITH sour cream, diced tomatoes, and fresh cilantro.

45

Cinnamon Roll Loaf

8 frozen cinnamon rolls *(from a 36.5 oz. pkg.)*, thawed but still cold*

Butter-flavored cooking spray

3 T. butter, melted, divided

1 tsp. cinnamon-sugar

1 icing pouch *(included in roll pkg.)*, thawed

Chopped pecans, optional

* Work with a few rolls at a time and keep the others refrigerated until ready to slice.

46

TO BEGIN, grease a 4½ x 8½" loaf pan with cooking spray and set aside.

Carefully slice each roll in half horizontally to make 16 thinner circles. Arrange the circles on a lightly floured surface, leaving space between them. Spritz circles with cooking spray and cover with plastic wrap. With a rolling pin, flatten the rolls into 4" rounds. Let rest in a warm place for 20 minutes.

Brush the rounds with some of the melted butter and stack the slices in bundles of three or four. Set the prepared pan up on one short side and place bundles in the pan *(there will be extra space)*. Turn pan upright and cover with sprayed waxed paper; let rise in a warm place about 50 minutes, carefully rearranging the rounds as needed partway through rising time to fill the pan more evenly.

Preheat the oven to 350°. Brush top of loaf with remaining melted butter and sprinkle with cinnamon-sugar. Bake 20 to 25 minutes or until golden brown and done in the center; tent with foil as needed to prevent overbrowning. Cool about 10 minutes before removing bread from pan. Drizzle the icing from pouch over the loaf.

GARNISH WITH pecans, if you'd like.

SOFT ITALIAN
Breadsticks

1 (¼ oz.) pkg. active dry yeast *(2¼ tsp.)*

1½ T. sugar, divided

¼ C. warm water *(105°-110°)*

1¼ C. warm milk *(100°)*

¼ C. plus 3 T. butter, softened, divided

2 tsp. salt

4 C. flour, divided, plus more for kneading

1½ to 2 tsp. Italian seasoning

1 tsp. garlic powder, or more to taste

¼ C. shredded Parmesan or Parmentino cheese

TO BEGIN, line an 11 x 15" rimmed baking sheet with parchment paper and set aside. To proof the yeast, stir together yeast, ½ tablespoon sugar, and warm water until mostly dissolved; let stand about 10 minutes until foamy.

In the bowl of an electric mixer with a dough hook, mix the warm milk, ¼ cup butter, salt, and remaining 1 tablespoon sugar. Mix in the yeast mixture. Add 3½ cups flour, ½ cup at a time, and mix well between additions until dough pulls away from the bowl. If dough seems too sticky, add more flour, a little at a time, up to 4 cups total. Turn dough out onto a floured board and knead 6 to 8 minutes, until smooth and elastic. Place in a greased bowl, turning once to grease the top. Cover with sprayed waxed paper and let rise in a warm place about 1½ hours, until doubled in size.

DIRECTIONS CONTINUED ·······························>

Pull-Aparts

48

Preheat the oven to 350°. Punch dough down and transfer to prepared baking sheet; press dough to fill pan. Slice into 24 strips, approximately 1¼ x 5½" long, but leave them in place *(cut the dough in half lengthwise and crosswise, and then make 10 evenly spaced crosswise cuts)*. Melt remaining 3 tablespoons butter and brush over dough. Sprinkle with Italian seasoning, garlic powder, and cheese. Bake 20 to 25 minutes or until lightly browned.

SERVE WITH your favorite dipping sauce.

49

CHERRY BISMARCK
Bloom

12 frozen white dinner rolls, thawed*

½ C. cherry jam, divided

2 T. sugar

3 T. finely ground slivered almonds

2 T. butter, melted

Almond Icing
(recipe follows)

TO BEGIN, line a 14" pizza pan with foil and grease with cooking spray. Flatten two thawed rolls into 3½" circles. Place 2 teaspoons jam between the circles and pinch edges together to seal. Set in the center of prepared pan.

Shape each remaining roll into an 8" log and fold in half to make an oval loop for each "flower petal." Press ends together and arrange petals evenly around filled center, edges touching. Lightly flatten the center of petals to close holes. Cover with sprayed waxed paper and let rise in a warm place 50 minutes or until doubled in size.

Mix sugar and almonds. Brush dough with melted butter and sprinkle with sugar mixture. Press a finger into each petal to enlarge dent; fill with a spoonful of jam. Bake 15 to 20 minutes or until golden brown. Let cool. Drizzle with Almond Icing.

ALMOND ICING Whisk together 1 C. powdered sugar, 1 tsp. almond flavoring, 1 T. melted butter, and 1 to 2 T. hot water or warm cream until smooth.

* Let thawed rolls rest at room temperature for 30 minutes before flattening.

51

MEXICAN JALAPEÑO
Cheddar Muffins

1 (16.3 oz.) tube refrigerated "grands" homestyle biscuits *(8 ct.)*

½ C. butter, melted

1 T. garlic powder

1 T. dried oregano

Deli-sliced jalapeños, drained well

1 C. shredded Mexican 4-cheese blend, divided

TO BEGIN, preheat the oven to 350°. Lightly grease 11 standard muffin cups and set aside.

Cut each biscuit into eight equal triangles. In a small bowl, stir together the melted butter, garlic powder, and oregano. Dip biscuit pieces in the butter mixture and place three pieces in each prepared muffin cup. Add a jalapeño slice and about 1 tablespoon cheese to each cup; top with three more biscuit pieces, another jalapeño slice, and remaining cheese. Bake 15 to 20 minutes or until golden brown.

SERVE WARM.

PULL-APART PIZZA

1 (13.8 oz.) tube refrigerated "classic" pizza dough

½ C. pizza sauce

1½ C. shredded mozzarella cheese, divided

20 pepperoni slices

1 T. butter, melted

½ tsp. garlic powder

2 T. grated Parmesan cheese

1 to 2 tsp. chopped fresh oregano

Coarse black pepper

Italian seasoning, optional

TO BEGIN, grease a 3½ x 7½" loaf pan with cooking spray and line the bottom with parchment paper, if desired.

Unroll the dough on a floured surface and flatten into a 12 x 16" rectangle. Spread sauce over dough and sprinkle with 1 cup mozzarella cheese. Arrange pepperoni over the cheese. Slice the dough crosswise into five even strips and then slice it lengthwise into four more strips to make 20 small squares. Stack the squares together in bundles of four. Set the prepared pan up on one short side and set bundles into the pan, filling side up *(flip the last square over, filling side down)*. Turn pan upright.

Preheat the oven to 400°. In a small bowl, mix melted butter and garlic powder. In another bowl, stir together Parmesan cheese, oregano, and pepper to taste; set bowls aside. Bake the bread about 40 minutes; remove from oven and brush with set-aside butter mixture. Sprinkle with remaining ½ cup mozzarella cheese, Parmesan mixture, and Italian seasoning, if you'd like. Return to oven to bake 5 to 10 minutes longer. Let cool about 10 minutes before removing from pan.

Ham & Cheese Stack

1 (16.3 oz.) tube refrigerated "grands" flaky biscuits *(8 ct.)*

6 T. mayonnaise

2 T. whole grain mustard

1 tsp. creamy horseradish

1 C. diced ham

8 oz. sliced cheese *(such as smoked Gouda or Swiss)*

1 T. butter, melted

¼ C. shredded Colby-Jack cheese

Sliced green onions

56

TO BEGIN, preheat the oven to 400°. Grease a
5 x 9" loaf pan with cooking spray and line the bottom
with parchment paper, if you'd like; set aside.

Slice or peel each biscuit in half to make 16 rounds.
Flatten the rounds into 3½" to 4" circles. In a small bowl,
mix the mayonnaise, mustard, and horseradish until well
blended; spread a spoonful on each biscuit round. Divide
the ham evenly among biscuits, pressing down lightly;
top with a slice of cheese, cutting to fit as needed. Set the
prepared pan up on one short side and stack the biscuits
in the pan with the filling side up *(flip the last biscuit over,
filling side down)*. Turn the pan upright and cover with foil.

Bake about 35 minutes. Remove foil and brush bread
with melted butter; sprinkle shredded cheese over the
top. Return to oven to bake uncovered 10 minutes more
or until cheese is melted and bread is deep golden
brown and done in the center. Let cool 10 minutes before
removing from pan. Serve promptly.

GARNISH WITH green onions for added zip.

57

COCONUT CREAM
Bubble Bread

18 frozen white dinner rolls, thawed but still cold

½ (3.5 oz.) pkg. coconut cream cook 'n' serve pudding mix *(about 5 T.)*

½ C. chopped pecans

½ C. butter

½ C. brown sugar

Toasted coconut, optional

TO BEGIN, grease a 10" Bundt pan with cooking spray. Cut each roll in half and coat well with the dry pudding mix. Arrange 12 coated roll pieces in the prepared pan. Sprinkle with ⅓ of the pecans. Repeat to make two more even layers with remaining rolls and nuts. Sprinkle any leftover pudding mix over the top.

Combine butter and brown sugar in a microwave-safe bowl and microwave on high for 1½ to 2 minutes, stirring after 1 minute. Stir again until smooth syrup forms; pour over ingredients in pan. Cover with sprayed waxed paper and let rise in a warm place 1 hour or until doubled in size.

Preheat the oven to 350°. Bake bread for 30 to 35 minutes. Cover lightly with foil for the last half of baking time to prevent overbrowning. Immediately loosen bread from the pan with a knife and invert onto a serving plate.

GARNISH WITH toasted coconut, if you'd like.

Pull-Aparts

58

59

SERVES 10

CHEESY BACON
& Garlic Pulls

1 (1 lb.) loaf Italian bread

½ C. butter, melted

1 tsp. garlic salt

4 oz. cream cheese, softened

1 T. minced garlic

2 C. shredded Colby-Jack cheese

1½ C. shredded Swiss cheese

8 bacon strips, cooked & crumbled

3 green onions, sliced

Chopped fresh parsley

Coarse black pepper

TO BEGIN, preheat the oven to 350°.

Cut bread in 1"-wide diagonal slices without cutting through the bottom crust. In the same way, cut diagonal slices in the opposite direction to make diamond-shaped pieces. Set the loaf on a large piece of foil. In a small bowl, combine melted butter and garlic salt. Brush butter mixture on all cut sides of bread and set aside.

In a medium bowl, beat cream cheese until smooth. Stir in the garlic, both shredded cheeses, and bacon until well combined. Stuff cheese mixture between all the cuts in bread. Wrap the loaf in foil and set it on a cookie sheet. Bake for 20 minutes. Open foil to uncover the bread; bake 10 to 15 minutes longer or until cheese is melted.

GARNISH WITH green onions, parsley, and pepper to taste before serving.

Pull-Aparts

60

PARMESAN TWISTS

1 (1 oz.) pkg. dry ranch
  dressing mix

2 (6.5 oz.) pkgs. pizza
  crust mix

Hot water as directed on
  crust mix packages

Vegetable oil

1 egg white, beaten

Coarse salt and black
  pepper to taste

3 to 4 T. grated Parmesan
  cheese

1 T. toasted sesame seed

TO BEGIN, grease a 14" round pizza pan with cooking spray; cut out a 12" parchment paper circle and set aside.

In a medium bowl, combine dressing mix and both crust mixes. Add the hot water as directed for each crust and stir until blended. Shape dough into a ball and brush with oil. Cover with sprayed waxed paper and let rise in a warm place for 15 minutes.

Preheat the oven to 400°. Place dough on the parchment paper circle and flatten until even with the edge of paper. Brush dough with egg white and sprinkle with salt, pepper, cheese, and sesame seed.

63

Mark a circle in the center of dough with the rim of a drinking glass. Starting at the outer edge and cutting to *(but not through)* the marked circle, slice the dough into 16 equal strips. Transfer the paper with dough to prepared pan. Twist each strip several times and stretch the ends toward the edge of pan; press down lightly. Bake 15 to 20 minutes or until golden brown.

SERVE WARM with your favorite dipping sauce.

Index

Pull-Aparts